WRITE EVERYDAY

A YEAR OF DAILY WRITING PROMPTS

WRITE EVERYDAY

A YEAR OF DAILY WRITING PROMPTS

BY J.M. SNYDER

WRITE EVERY DAY: A YEAR OF DAILY WRITING PROMPTS

JMS Books LLC
10286 Staples Mill Rd. #221
Glen Allen, VA 23060
www.jms-books.com

ISBN: 9781480176683

Printed in the United States of America

INTRODUCTION

AS A WRITER, I love prompts that jumpstart my muse and get the creative juices flowing. Sometimes I want to write and don't really know what I should write about, and prompts help guide me into a new story. I've written many stories that began as an interesting prompt in a writing class or author group, and then grew to take on a life of its own.

But I'm frequently disappointed with books of writing prompts because while they're creative and inspiring, I find it very difficult to settle on any one prompt to work on at a time. I'll find something, think it sounds good, then flip the page and find another prompt that looks just as promising, then turn to *another* page...you get the drift. I'm easily distracted, and would rather read through the entire book of prompts rather than pick one out at random and write.

When I began this book, I decided to eliminate that indecisiveness, in case other writers suffer from it as well. I thought if I wrote the book in a diary or planner format, with one prompt per day for an entire year, then it would be a no-brainer which prompt to use. Whatever day it happens to be, flip to that page, and viola! Instant inspiration.

The idea, of course, is to write everyday. It's only by writing that one becomes a writer, and practice makes perfect. Even if you aren't working on a particular story, writing a brief scene or a short thousand-word story is a great way to stay in shape and hone your writing ability. It also gets you into a routine, and writing daily will sooner or later lead to a finished story or book.

This collection of writing prompts can be used on a daily basis. Every day turn the page to the new prompt, set a timer for fifteen or twenty minutes, and write wherever the prompt takes you. Or, if you're between stories and looking for something different to work on, flip to the prompt for today and start fresh.

The prompts in this collection are my own creations. They're inspired by things I've seen or experienced in my own life. Many times throughout the day I think, "What if…?" The writer in me never turns off, and on an average day, I'll get dozen of story or scene ideas. Unfortunately, I know I'll probably never be able to write out all of them—most I forget after a few minutes, and I figure in that case they probably weren't very good to start with. But hopefully these prompts will help trigger your own stories and get you writing—or, if you're already writing on a daily basis, keep you going.

There are several types of prompts in this book. Some start simply, "Write a story about…" or "Write about someone who…" Others present a question you should answer through the story you decide to tell. And many are scenarios presented in the second person, where "you" can be anyone you want—male or female, gay or straight, young or old, human or not. I kept these deliberately vague to allow your imagination to kick into overdrive. These prompts can be used to write stories in any genre you prefer, be it contemporary, sci-fi or fantasy, horror, romance, erotica, paranormal…whatever tickles your fancy.

I hope you'll find these prompts useful in kick-starting your writing or taking your current stories in exciting new directions. They were a lot of fun for me to write. I hope they're just as fun for you to use as fodder for your next story!

J.M. Snyder
December 2012

JANUARY 1

It's New Year's Day.
You make a resolution, which you promptly break.

JANUARY 2

Something happens that sends you hurrying
to an emergency veterinary clinic.

JANUARY 3

Tell a ghost story from the ghost's point of view.

ꟙ

JANUARY 4

You're walking through a park or along a nature trail when you stumble upon something you've read about but have never seen.

JANUARY 5

Imagine a world where, instead of rain,
something else falls as precipitation from the sky.
Describe how it feels to live in such a world.

JANUARY 6

You have the winning numbers
to the multi-million dollar state lottery,
but for some reason, you can't find the ticket.

JANUARY 7

One day, by accident, you discover you can fly.

JANUARY 8

You somehow get trapped in a favorite video game or a frequently used smartphone app.

JANUARY 9

You're asked to pet sit for an acquaintance over the weekend, but you don't know what type of pet it will be. When you arrive at the house, you're surprise to find out.

JANUARY 10

One morning, you wake up and look in the bathroom mirror, but something is different about your reflection.

JANUARY 11

You are a world-renowned chef in a cook-off competition who's asked to work with an ingredient you normally refuse to cook.

ꙮ

JANUARY 12

You go to see your favorite band perform live in concert, but get lost trying to find your seat and wind up backstage, where you run into the band's lead singer.

JANUARY 13

Even in this digital age, you still have a subscription to the local newspaper. One morning when you open to the front page, you see the paper is dated a week into the future. And the cover story on the front page is terrifying.

ᘓᘐ

JANUARY 14

You get a wedding invitation from someone who used to be your best friend back in school. But the name of your friend's future spouse is *also* familiar to you…for a bad reason.

JANUARY 15

You are a coach or teacher who accidentally discovers your star pupil has been cheating. No one else knows.

JANUARY 16

While looking through an old school yearbook, you come across a note from a former friend that surprises you.

JANUARY 17

You're offered the chance to attain the one thing you want most in this world—any one thing, a job or person or ability, anything. But if you take it, something dire will happen (not death, at least, not for you).

JANUARY 18

You find a cell phone, but before you can turn it over to the rightful owner, it rings. You answer, and the person on the other end says, "I did what you told me to, so where's my money?"

JANUARY 19

As a child, you were always afraid something bad was hiding in your closet. When you return to your childhood home as an adult, you take a look in the closet to alleviate your fears only to find out you were right all along. There *is* something in there.

JANUARY 20

You receive a notice that you've won an award for something you didn't do, but you know who did.

JANUARY 21

The person of your dreams asks you out. But once on the date, you realize the person thinks you're someone else. You can either come clean or go along with it, but at some point you run into someone who knows who you really are.

JANUARY 22

Someone at a child's birthday party has killed someone just before arriving. No one else knows yet. What happens when the police arrive at the house on an unrelated matter?

JANUARY 23

Write about someone with a unique, exciting, or adventurous job who hates what they do. *Examples*: pirate, movie star, President of the United States, cowboy, fashion model, spaceship pilot, pop star.

ഈ ഗ

JANUARY 24

You're online looking at wedding rings in the hope of proposing to your significant other when you notice that person's Facebook status has just been updated to "Single and Looking."

JANUARY 25

You see a cat playing with a squeaky toy. On closer inspection, you discover the "toy" is really a fairy. And it's alive.

ꟸ

JANUARY 26

You're doing something you don't want anyone else to see. You think you're alone in the house when you hear a sneeze from the next room.

JANUARY 27

You live in an apartment with thin walls, allowing you to hear your neighbors well. One night, you overhear an argument next door that escalates into violence. A gunshot rings out. Before you can react, your phone rings.

JANUARY 28

It's your birthday, but someone important to you forgets.

JANUARY 29

You're doing laundry when you find a pair of underwear that doesn't belong to you.

JANUARY 30

You're a salesman peddling a product you despise. One day, you decide to let everyone know just how much you hate this item.

JANUARY 31

You have some sort of physical ailment (headache, toothache, bruise) that keeps getting worse. When you finally go to the doctor, you're told, "I wish you'd come in sooner."

FEBRUARY 1

It's snowing badly, and you're stuck somewhere in public with two people—one you like a lot, and one you can't stand.

FEBRUARY 2

You find an old map of your hometown that seems to lead to treasure. Looking it over, you realize you know exactly where X marks the spot. It's a place you know well.

FEBRUARY 3

You come home one day to find something missing from your home. Everything else is in order and the house wasn't broken into.

FEBRUARY 4

You have a really inconvenient, almost embarrassing, superpower.

FEBRUARY 5

You find a ransom note in your mailbox that was delivered to the wrong address and is clearly intended for someone else.

FEBRUARY 6

You wake up one day to discover you seem to be
the only person left in the world.
Everyone else has disappeared.

FEBRUARY 7

You work in a profession where your ability
to predict the future comes in handy.

FEBRUARY 8

You open a can of food to eat but are surprised to find what's inside isn't what you were expecting.

FEBRUARY 9

While out of town on business or vacation, you remember something important you forgot—or forgot to do—back home.

FEBRUARY 10

You receive a letter from an old friend whom you haven't heard from in years. The letter begins, "You're the only person who knows about the time we…"

FEBRUARY 11

Tell a story about a celebrity or famous person (real or imaginary, contemporary or historical) from the point of view of that person's pampered pet.

FEBRUARY 12

Write about someone's first experience with death.

FEBRUARY 13

You're asked to do something you don't want to do, so you decide to trick someone else into doing it for you.

FEBRUARY 14

It's Valentine's Day, and you aren't expecting anyone to send you anything. So you're surprised when a beautiful bouquet of flowers arrives at the office for you with a mysterious note.

FEBRUARY 15

A sports car runs into a minivan at a stop light. Write the scene from the point of view of the driver of the sports car Then write the same scene from the point of view of someone inside the minivan.

FEBRUARY 16

What's the first thing you kiss in the morning?

FEBRUARY 17

Why would you buy a box of baby wipes
if you had no small children?

FEBRUARY 18

You're going about your normal daily routine when you see an exotic animal where one shouldn't be.

FEBRUARY 19

Write about a society in which something necessary to life (other than food) is rationed by the government.

FEBRUARY 20

You hear a mysterious sound in your home and track it down to an unlikely source.

FEBRUARY 21

Write a story that starts when you've finished digging a hole in the backyard. Working from the end, retrace what happened until you get to the beginning, where you discover you have to dig the hole. Make this the end of your story.

FEBRUARY 22

You want something just out of reach
(physically, not metaphorically).

FEBRUARY 23

Write about someone pretending to be something they are not.

FEBRUARY 24

You order something online for a special event (birthday or wedding gift, trade show items, books for a signing). The package arrives just as you're leaving to go to the event, so you don't have time to open and inspect its contents. When you reach your destination and finally open the package, you find you were shipped the wrong thing.

FEBRUARY 25

It's the end of February. In the northern hemisphere, it's winter, but below the equator, summer is coming to an end. Write about someone in February who lives in a part of the world opposite, weather-wise, from what it's like where you currently live.

FEBRUARY 26

You're on some sort of public transportation
(train, bus, plane) for a long ride when you notice
an ex-lover sitting a few seats away.

FEBRUARY 27

Tell a story centering around a family recipe.
Feel free to include the recipe in the story or at the end!

FEBRUARY 28

While caring for an elderly female relative (mother, grandmother, older aunt), you discover she has a tattoo you never noticed before.

ജ ഉ

FEBRUARY 29

Almost 10,000 birds die every year from smashing into windows. Write about someone who witnesses such an accident, but the bird survives.

MARCH 1

Write about someone with an ordinary, almost boring, job who works in an unusual or exotic place. *Examples*: plumber at a space station, receptionist at the White House, cashier at a shop at the Olympics.

MARCH 2

One day you find a closed door where you've never seen one before. When you pass by, it opens.

MARCH 3

While at work, you call home to say you'll be working late, but a stranger answers the phone.

MARCH 4

You're a celebrity about to walk on stage in front of a live audience. This performance is being broadcast live on television and streaming online at the same time. You plan to make a stunning announcement no one else knows about in advance.

MARCH 5

You get into a car that looks like yours but isn't.

MARCH 6

You're in court on a false accusation. Describe the hearing. For a twist, the judge finds you guilty even though you aren't.

MARCH 7

Something you post or tweet online gets you called into your boss's office.

MARCH 8

Write about someone who always takes an animal with them when they leave the house.

MARCH 9

You pick up a copy of the big best-selling novel everyone's talking about only to find it's copied word for word from an unpublished manuscript of yours that's been in your files for years.

MARCH 10

Write about a person who is perfectly ordinary in every single way but one.

MARCH 11

Write about someone who wants to buy
a large order of dandelion seeds.

MARCH 12

You find an unfamiliar key.

MARCH 13

You wake up one day suddenly unable to see one particular color. Which? How do you notice it's gone?

ᔓᔕ

MARCH 14

You administer drug tests at a lab. Write a scene in which you suspect someone is trying to skew the test results.

MARCH 15

Write about entering the Oval Office at the White House
for the first time.

MARCH 16

You meet a sibling for the first time.

MARCH 17

You're an adult who collects a particular type of children's toy.
Write about an attempt to get a special item
to complete your collection.

MARCH 18

You come home one day to find every light
in the house has been turned on.

MARCH 19

Write about someone trying to explain "the birds and the bees" to a child. Mix it up—make the characters different genders. Maybe the adult is gay and the child questions his or her about their sexuality.

MARCH 20

It's after midnight and you're in bed when your phone rings. The friend calling says, "I need you to come quick."

MARCH 21

Write about someone who decides to get
a tattoo for the first time.

MARCH 22

Modernize an old fairy tale.
Does Cinderella have a shoe fetish?
Is Beauty's Beast a werewolf?
Take a favorite tale and re-imagine it.

MARCH 23

Write about someone addicted to something (it doesn't have to be drugs or alcohol, or anything illicit) who has run out of the item and needs a "fix."

ᛟ

MARCH 24

You are left a large inheritance in a family will, but only if you do something you don't want to do.

MARCH 25

Write a scene where someone is hiding behind the shower curtain when another person comes in to use the bathroom.

ꟾ

MARCH 26

You hear a large, concussive *BOOM!*, then feel the earth rumble. What just happened?

MARCH 27

Write a story in which the only relationship is between a human and a machine. It can be any type of machine (computer, household appliance, smartphone, robot).

MARCH 28

Write a story about someone who takes riding lessons for the first time. It doesn't have to be on a horse.

MARCH 29

As an adult, you meet a childhood idol of yours.

MARCH 30

You go on a horrible first date with someone you really like. Everything that can go wrong, does. Describe the date in detail.

MARCH 31

You find a photo online which makes you suspect your spouse is having an affair.

APRIL 1

While looking at Google street maps of your neighborhood, you discover what appears to be a photograph of a crime being committed.

APRIL 2

Write a story about a particular smell or scent that evokes an extreme emotion (good or bad). Describe it in such detail, your readers can smell it, too.

APRIL 3

Write a story about a sport from the point of view of someone who doesn't like it.

APRIL 4

You have an unusual phobia. Describe the fear, where it stems from, and how you react when you have to face it.

ᵹᘐ

APRIL 5

You try to do something for the first time—and discover you really have a knack for it!

APRIL 6

You're granted three wishes, but you don't find the genie in a bottle. Where is it? What do you wish for?

APRIL 7

Write about someone forced to live without power for some reason (Storm outage? Safari or camping trip? Visiting an Amish friend? Zombie apocalypse? You decide!). What frustrates them the most? What do they miss without electricity?

APRIL 8

One day you wake up as—or discover you can turn into—some sort of animal. Don't pick werewolf, that's too common. Think of something unusual.

APRIL 9

You fail a driving test. Describe what happened.

APRIL 10

You're dining with a friend and offer to pick up the tab. You discover the waiter has written a personal message to you on the bottom of the bill.

APRIL 11

You wake up in a dingy basement, chained to the wall. Two of your best friends are also held prisoner in the same room. The door opens, and you're surprised to discover you know exactly who your captor is. But why are you being held captive?

APRIL 12

You're running for office, and at a public debate, you swear to take a hard stand on a particularly volatile issue. When someone in the audience questions you about it, you're shocked to recognize the person. You haven't seen him or her in years, and you know they have dirt on you that might cost you the election.

APRIL 13

Someone gives you a horrible birthday present. What is it? How do you react? What do you do with the gift?

APRIL 14

You go back in time and find yourself on the deck of the *RMS Titanic* a few hours before it strikes an iceberg and founders. Can you save the ship?

APRIL 15

You decide to cheat on your income taxes this year. Why? How? And do you get caught?

APRIL 16

Retell a classic fairy tale from the point of view of the story's villain or "bad guy" (such as the evil witch, the troll, the pied piper).

ஐ CS

APRIL 17

You have a very unusual name. Write a scene where you're introduced to several people, each of whom comments on your name until you're tired of hearing the same silly things over and over again.

APRIL 18

An Olympic athlete (in the sport of your choice) has an intense rivalry with a member of his own team that almost costs them the gold.

APRIL 19

Rewrite a familiar nursery rhyme as a story told from the point of view of one of the characters.

APRIL 20

Write about someone flying for the first time.
It doesn't have to be in a plane.

APRIL 21

You print something personal to the wrong office printer at work. When you go to retrieve it, you find someone else has already picked it up.

APRIL 22

Choose a favorite movie or book and write a story from the point of view of a minor character who doesn't have much to do or say in the original story.

APRIL 23

You're in an elevator with someone else when the power goes out.

APRIL 24

You wake in the middle of the night to noises made by your pet, who is obviously upset and bothered by something.

APRIL 25

A week after attending a very touching funeral, you get a text from the deceased that reads, "I'm not dead."

APRIL 26

Write about someone who receives a sex toy catalogue they didn't order.

APRIL 27

Write a scene in which you get really happy or excited about something no one else cares about.

APRIL 28

You meet someone online and start to fall for them, but when you meet in real life, you're surprised to discover who your online crush turns out to be.

APRIL 29

Your best friend asks for help killing someone. You agree. Write the story as a dark comedy.

APRIL 30

You're a hairdresser who purposefully gives someone a horrible hair cut.

MAY 1

You have a particularly dangerous or risky job. Write a story describing a typical work day.

MAY 2

While watching an adult film, you recognize one of the actors as someone you know in real life.

MAY 3

You're in a steady relationship with someone who likes to go with you on dates to weird or unusual places.

MAY 4

Your upstairs neighbor is usually very quiet, but one night it's so noisy up there, you go to investigate.

MAY 5

A car alarm wakes you up in the middle of the night. When you investigate, you discover it isn't your car but the one beside it. What's happening?

MAY 6

You have an odd hobby usually done at home alone to pass the time (such as knitting, crossword puzzles, or scrapbooking). Imagine a national competition in that "event." Describe your participation in it.

MAY 7

You're driving behind someone who isn't driving very well (swerving, going too slow, etc.). But when you finally pass the other car, you glance over and see something's going on in the front seat that's distracting the driver.

MAY 8

You get a call from a friend who says, "You have to come with me. You're the only other person with a key."

MAY 9

You work at a museum (real or fictional) which is haunted. While you're familiar with the ghost stories, some of your visitors aren't. Write a scene where you witness ghostly activity while taking some skeptical visitors on a guided tour.

MAY 10

Write about a society just like today's high tech world except dinosaurs never went extinct.

MAY 11

You're trapped somewhere during a disaster with a favorite pet and a neighbor you always though was annoying. When food runs low, the neighbor suggests you eat the pet. You refuse. Write this scene.

MAY 12

Write a story in which the only relationship is between a human and an animal (it doesn't have to be a pet, or even tame).

ꙮ

MAY 13

You throw a party and intentionally don't invite a particular person. But, to your surprise, that person shows up anyway.

MAY 14

You're a magician who forgets how a magic trick is supposed to work halfway through your performance.

ꙮ

MAY 15

You find something growing in your garden that shouldn't be there.

MAY 16

Write a story in which you meet, find, or communicate with an alien life form.

MAY 17

Write about someone who's excited about attending a science fiction convention.

MAY 18

Write a scene about the first time you held
the first book you published.

MAY 19

A scientist discovers a cure for cancer,
but it has one horrible side effect.

MAY 20

You have something in your car you don't want anyone else to see. It doesn't have to be anything illegal. You're driving home when you're stopped by police. Describe what happens.

MAY 21

Two friends who haven't seen each other in years meet up at their high school reunion. When they go out for drinks afterwards, one of the friends tells the other a deep, dark secret he or she has never shared before.

MAY 22

Write about someone who decides to visit
a fortune teller or voodoo priest or priestess.

ꟸꟷ

MAY 23

Write a scene in which someone admits to
another person that he or she is gay.

MAY 24

You're single but win a romantic getaway trip for two to an exotic location you've always dreamed of visiting. Who do you get to go with you? Describe how you ask this person and what happens on the trip when everyone assumes you two are a couple.

MAY 25

Three people take a trip somewhere, but only two return.

MAY 26

During heavy traffic, you're at a standstill on a tall bridge when you notice someone who looks like they're going to jump.

ഌരം

MAY 27

You're in the grocery store with a young child (your own or a relative, or someone you're babysitting) and get distracted. When you look around for the child, you realize he or she is gone.

MAY 28

Write a scene in which someone gets stuck
in a public restroom stall.

MAY 29

You wake up one morning with the ability to read minds.

MAY 30

You sneak into a swimming pool after hours only to discover what appears to be a body floating in the deep end of the pool.

ꟸ

MAY 31

While visiting your date's parents for the first time, you're served something for dinner that you really hate to eat.

JUNE 1

Lying in bed alone at night, you're almost asleep when you hear someone else draw in a breath beside you.

JUNE 2

You're on a plane when, in mid-flight, you notice a very sick passenger across the aisle from you.

JUNE 3

You wake up to find someone—or something—in your bed
that wasn't there when you went to sleep
and shouldn't be there now.

ഗ്ര

JUNE 4

You gain recognition or win a major literary award
for a work you know you plagiarized.

JUNE 5

You're at a family dinner reminiscing with your relatives when you begin to realize their memories of shared events aren't the same as yours.

JUNE 6

While touring an empty open house, you realize you've been inside the home before, and not under pleasant circumstances.

JUNE 7

You're walking along the beach when you see something strange in the waves.

JUNE 8

You're a reporter who, as a joke, writes up an outrageously fake news story. Then, to your surprise, what you "reported" really happens.

JUNE 9

Write a scene in which someone tells another person she's pregnant.

JUNE 10

Upon entering a dark room, you reach to turn on the light when a hand covers yours.

JUNE 11

You discover the glass gazing globe in your garden is really a crystal ball that can show you the future.

JUNE 12

Write about a divorced couple who decide to get married to each other again.

JUNE 13

Write about a ritual you have to perform before—or after—doing something you frequently do (such as go to bed).

ഌൡ

JUNE 14

You reconnect with an old friend online and agree to meet for lunch. When you arrive, you notice something about your friend has changed dramatically, and you're afraid to mention it.

JUNE 15

You're called in for a job interview but, at some point, notice
the interviewer is reading from the wrong resume.
It isn't yours, but you really want or need this job,
so you decide not to mention it.

ഇ ഗ

JUNE 16

You're in the shower when the water cuts off.

JUNE 17

You're in the car in a parking lot waiting on a friend when someone you don't know comes up to your window and says, "I need to go to the hospital right now!"

ജ ☙

JUNE 18

Write a story set in the past in which something modern is available then. *Examples*: smartphones during the Civil War, cameras at the Salem Witch Trials, the internet in King Arthur's Court, machine guns in Colonial times.

JUNE 19

You make a bet with a friend that you have every intention of losing.

ꝏ

JUNE 20

It won't stop raining.

JUNE 21

Write a scene in which someone *has* to get into a stranger's car against their better judgment.

JUNE 22

You're leaving on a lengthy military deployment. Describe the scene in which you say goodbye to your significant other.

JUNE 23

You don't believe in New Age or homeopathic remedies, but something convinces you such treatments work.

JUNE 24

Write a story about someone who has dreams of running to or from something…or someone.

JUNE 25

According to the United States Postal Service, you can mail a coconut with only a stamp and a mailing address. Write about someone who receives a coconut in the mail.

JUNE 26

While researching your family tree, you discover you're related to a notorious person in history.

JUNE 27

On average, twelve newborns are given to the wrong parents every day. Write about someone who, later in life, discovers that he or she is one of them.

ജ്ക

JUNE 28

Write a story in which someone celebrates an anniversary alone.

JUNE 29

Write a story where something happens (or doesn't happen) when someone who is very superstitious fails to observe a particular superstition.

JUNE 30

Write a story set in a child's room from the point of view of one of the child's toys.

JULY 1

You're being held hostage during a bank robbery when your cell phone rings.

JULY 2

Write a story from the point of view of someone waiting for a loved one in the military to return from a tour of duty.

JULY 3

Think of your favorite song. Without quoting any lyrics, tell a story inspired by the song.

JULY 4

Write about someone who is just about to give up hope when the sight of a flag rallies their strength and conviction.

JULY 5

Write about someone learning to drive for the first time.
It doesn't have to be a car.

JULY 6

In a crowded club one Friday night, your friends convince you to ask out the very next person who walks by.

JULY 7

While enjoying a drink or meal alone in public, you slowly begin to realize someone is watching you.

JULY 8

You're staying in a hotel room for a weekend getaway and discover a bloody knife sticking out from under the bed.

JULY 9

Write a scene in which someone you love deeply admits to you that he or she is gay.

ꙮ

JULY 10

A bike messenger or courier who stops by your office on his daily route always flirts with you, but when you get up the nerve to invite him out to lunch, he declines.

JULY 11

You're in the waiting room of a clinic, waiting on test results.

ꕥ

JULY 12

Write a story about someone who can actually smell fear.

JULY 13

Your pet dog digs up what appears to be a human leg bone from your backyard.

ജ്ഞ

JULY 14

Write about someone who works in an art museum and begins a love affair (real or imagined) with one of the paintings.

JULY 15

You're a backup singer on tour with a famous superstar when he or she falls ill and you're asked to perform instead.

ᘓᘐ

JULY 16

While eating, you think you break a tooth only to discover what looks like part of a microchip inside your mouth.

JULY 17

You find a stash of feminine items such as make-up, hair spray, and bras while cleaning out your son's bedroom.

ꕥ

JULY 18

Random items disappear from your bachelor pad apartment, even though you're the only one with a key.

JULY 19

It's winter in the southern hemisphere.
Write about someone used to summer heat who visits a place where it usually snows in July.

ജ ഌ

JULY 20

At a place you frequently eat lunch, one day you notice something new—and strange—on the menu.

JULY 21

A backyard cookout takes a turn for the worst when the gas canister beneath the grill explodes.

ꕥ

JULY 22

Write a story from the point of view of a mythical or mythological creature, being, or deity who lives in today's society.

JULY 23

Write about someone who donated sperm while in college only to be tracked down by one of his biological children years later.

ഇ ശ

JULY 24

Finding an old brochure stirs up nostalgic or melancholic feelings.

JULY 25

You agree to give a presentation on a topic you're familiar with at an upcoming members' meeting. You just didn't expect the members to be dressing in S&M and bondage gear.

ജ ഗ

JULY 26

Write a story about someone along on a midnight ghost hunt who doesn't believe in the supernatural.

JULY 27

Write a story about a local food festival from the point of view of one of the cooks who hopes to take home the winning prize.

ഇ ഗ

JULY 28

While drunk, you decide to prank call someone in another country.

JULY 29

You find an old family cookbook, but to your surprise, instead of recipes, it contains magical spells.

ℵ ℑ

JULY 30

You're making dinner for your spouse's boss and everything is just about ready to serve when you realize you left out a very important ingredient.

JULY 31

You log online one day to find your website or Facebook account has been hacked…and you think you know by whom.

ᘓᘐ

AUGUST 1

An employee of yours is out sick for several days before you begin to suspect he or she was killed by the spouse who's been calling in for them.

AUGUST 2

It's one of the hottest days of the year, but when you drive past a bank sign displaying the temperature, you're shocked to see it read 129° F!

AUGUST 3

Write about someone interested in vacationing on the moon.

AUGUST 4

When you learn your best friend has been hospitalized after a car crash, you have to get into his or her apartment to hide something before the friend's parents arrive, but you don't have a key.

ஐ

AUGUST 5

While pumping gas, you witness a robbery in progress that you think is just a joke at first.

AUGUST 6

Write a story about someone who catches a pop-up fly ball at a local baseball game.

AUGUST 7

You and your coworkers are goofing off on the job when your boss comes over and asks to join in.

AUGUST 8

Write a story involving a cell phone, a hundred dollar bill, and an ice cream truck.

AUGUST 9

When you open your usual box of breakfast cereal one morning, you find something unusual inside.

AUGUST 10

Only 5% of people shot in the head survive.
Write a story about one of them.

AUGUST 11

Something convinces you that your computer or smartphone has developed an intelligent mind of its own.

AUGUST 12

When a hurricane blows through town, you find yourself trapped in your car on the interstate, which has been shut down due to flooding. As you prepare to wait out the storm, you notice someone stranded on the shoulder who needs help before being washed away.

AUGUST 13

Someone you know mistakenly sends you a sexy text.

AUGUST 14

When you meet your favorite author at a book signing, he or she slips you their phone number when they sign your book.

ᘓᘐ

AUGUST 15

Write about someone who cuts themselves badly but decides not to go to the doctor right away.

AUGUST 16

You're traveling along the interstate and stop at a rest area to relieve yourself. When you return to your car, you find a note on your windshield that reads, "Help me!"

AUGUST 17

You're walking home in bad weather because your car broke down when someone you think doesn't like you stops to offer you a ride.

AUGUST 18

Write a story about someone who is superstitious about a particular number and how that impacts their daily routine. It doesn't have to be unlucky—it can be a lucky number, a birthday, a player's jersey number, or just a favorite number.

AUGUST 19

While you're house sitting for someone away on vacation, something happens that forces you to call them immediately the next time you check on the house.

AUGUST 20

Write a story about a machine or robot
that falls in love with a human.

AUGUST 21

As a joke, you make a list of coworkers (or teachers, or fellow students, or celebrities) in the order in which you think they will die. To your surprise and growing horror, your "death list" predictions start to come true.

AUGUST 22

Write about someone who has to stay at a hotel for more than a month.

AUGUST 23

Write about someone who can remember in vivid detail exactly where they were or what they were doing when they learned that a particular celebrity had died.

AUGUST 24

Someone tells you that your home is built on an ancient burial ground, and your response is, "That explains it!" Explains what?

AUGUST 25

You come home one day to find a police car parked in front of your house.

AUGUST 26

Write a scene in which a homeschooled child or teenager argues with his or her parents about being allowed to attend public school.

AUGUST 27

Write a story about someone who is happy summer is over.

AUGUST 28

You live in an apartment building and think you overhear your neighbor kill someone in a fit of rage. Instead of going to the police, you decide to blackmail him or her into paying for your silence.

AUGUST 29

While cleaning out an old closet, you discover a panel in the ceiling that opens to reveal an attic you didn't know you had.

AUGUST 30

While on vacation, you accidentally find a creature long believed to be extinct.

AUGUST 31

You win a national recipe contest using an item you didn't make from scratch but rather purchased from a local store.

SEPTEMBER 1

Write a story about someone who is going back to school.

SEPTEMBER 2

You sign up for a cruise that sails through the Bermuda Triangle.

SEPTEMBER 3

Airplane lights you see in the night sky turn out to belong to a UFO.

SEPTEMBER 4

Write about someone who begs for money at an intersection of a busy street, but isn't what they seem to be at first glance.

SEPTEMBER 5

You're interviewing candidates for a position in your firm. The next applicant went to school with you and you remember them well, but they don't recognize you. Make it someone you knew, such as a secret crush or a schoolyard bully. Describe the interview.

SEPTEMBER 6

You're sleeping when the sound of someone entering your home with a key wakes you up. You don't recognize the person.

SEPTEMBER 7

One day when you log online to update your blog, you find unpublished draft posts written by someone else…
and addressed to you.

SEPTEMBER 8

Write a story inspired by an urban legend.

SEPTEMBER 9

While working late at a convenience store, you're robbed at gunpoint by someone you know.

SEPTEMBER 10

You rave over a friend's signature dish only to be surprised or shocked when he or she tells you what the "secret" ingredient is.

SEPTEMBER 11

Write about someone who's nervous to be flying on 9/11.

SEPTEMBER 12

E-books you didn't purchase begin showing up on your handheld e-reader (Kindle, Nook, iPad, etc).

SEPTEMBER 13

Write a story about someone wearing a dog collar
(either by force or by choice).

SEPTEMBER 14

You're a magician who somehow manages to make someone *really* disappear…and you don't know how to get them back.

SEPTEMBER 15

You're on a date at the movies but when the film ends, you find someone else sitting beside you instead of the person you came in with.

SEPTEMBER 16

Write about someone who aspires to be in the Guinness Book of World Records for something weird or unusual.

SEPTEMBER 17

Write a scene in which someone can't stop checking his or her email, no matter how mad it makes someone else.

ഇ ര

SEPTEMBER 18

Bored with your current relationship, you answer a personals ad. This new person sounds exciting and fun, but when you arrive at the restaurant where you agree to meet, you see your current beau already seated and apparently waiting for someone.

SEPTEMBER 19

You decide to switch jobs when you turn forty and finally follow the dream you'd always put off before.

ᘓᘐ

SEPTEMBER 20

Write about someone who accidentally wins a contest or title at school or work that is obviously based on popularity.

SEPTEMBER 21

You're visiting an old home when you notice a portrait of someone whose eyes seem to follow you around the room.

SEPTEMBER 22

Write about someone who goes to a masseuse only to be surprised it's someone they already know…and don't particularly like.

SEPTEMBER 23

You're in a room or area that seems to be infested by a particular type of insect.

SEPTEMBER 24

Write a story that takes place entirely in the back seat of a taxi cab.

SEPTEMBER 25

Why would an adult be sleeping with the light on?

SEPTEMBER 26

You put a seashell to your ear, but instead of the ocean, you hear something surprisingly different.

SEPTEMBER 27

When shredding old bills, you accidentally destroy an important document.

SEPTEMBER 28

Write a story about someone who wakes up handcuffed to someone else.

SEPTEMBER 29

Write about someone who one day decides not to go back to their job ever again.

SEPTEMBER 30

You wake up to discover your hair color has changed dramatically overnight.

OCTOBER 1

You won a lot of money on a game show, but on your way home, you're kidnapped by someone who wants half your earnings or he'll tell authorities how you cheated on the show.

OCTOBER 2

While surfing the Internet, you learn your spouse has a fake persona they use online.

OCTOBER 3

Write a story about a person who arrives at a party with someone but leaves with someone else.

OCTOBER 4

Write about someone who gets shot.

OCTOBER 5

Write a story about someone who continuously steals from their place of employment.

OCTOBER 6

You're a celebrity who returns to your small hometown for your high school reunion.

OCTOBER 7

You get an email from someone you know
has been dead for over a year.

OCTOBER 8

Your new glasses give you X-ray vision.

OCTOBER 9

You accidentally break something you know a relative you live with will be very upset about.

OCTOBER 10

Why would an adult carry a large stuffed animal through an airport security checkpoint?

OCTOBER 11

Write a story about someone who works at the
dream job they always wanted and hates it.

OCTOBER 12

Write a scene in which someone has to fire their best friend
from a job, duty, or position.

OCTOBER 13

Write a story about a sports game of your choice from the point of view of the person inside the home team's mascot suit.

ହ୦ଓ

OCTOBER 14

Write about a member of royalty (king, queen, prince/ss, etc.) who doesn't live in a castle, palace, or mansion.

OCTOBER 15

After a series of strange events, you begin to suspect someone close to you was abducted by aliens and replaced with a robot or clone.

OCTOBER 16

On your birthday, you receive a card from an old friend you haven't spoken with in years. Inside is a note that reads, "Call me," and, to your surprise, the phone number is local.

OCTOBER 17

When driving on a deserted stretch of road one night, you catch a glimpse of something unbelievable in your headlights.

ᘛᘚ

OCTOBER 18

The pills you're taking for a head cold give you an unexpected superpower as a side effect.

OCTOBER 19

What appears to be a large bird of prey flying overheard is, on closer inspection, an angel following you.

OCTOBER 20

Write about someone who's desperately trying to get a signal on their phone or computer.

OCTOBER 21

Why would you go to the store as soon as it opened?
Or to an all-night store in the wee hours of the morning?

OCTOBER 22

Write about an author or reporter on deadline who's unable to write due to a horrible case of writer's block.

OCTOBER 23

You hear a knock on the door and, when you answer it, there stands the Grim Reaper of Death. After a few moments of conversation, though, he says, "My bad, wrong address."

OCTOBER 24

You're driving on an empty road when you see a limo or bus broken down on the shoulder. Someone flags you down. When you stop, you realize the vehicle belongs to today's hottest pop star who needs a ride to the venue where they'll be performing that evening.

OCTOBER 25

You return to your hometown years after leaving.
Describe how it's changed and how it's stayed the same.

OCTOBER 26

Write a story about someone with a tattoo
they think somehow communicates with them.

OCTOBER 27

The night after attending a Halloween party, you wake up to find you've turned into the costume you wore.

ନ୍ଦ

OCTOBER 28

Your Halloween costume doesn't suit the weather. If it's cold outside, your costume is too skimpy; if it's unseasonably warm, your costume is bulky and hot. Write about your evening in the uncomfortable getup.

OCTOBER 29

At a Halloween party, you become interested in someone wearing a mask or costume that keeps their identity a secret. You get pretty intimate at the party, but the next day when they call you, you're surprised to find you already know each other, and you would've never given that person your number if you'd known who they were at the time.

OCTOBER 30

You attend a Halloween party in costume only to find someone else is wearing the same thing as you. Worse, everyone at the party has difficulty telling you two apart!

OCTOBER 31

Write about a real supernatural creature
(vampire, werewolf, ghost) who takes his or her child
trick-or-treating on Halloween.

NOVEMBER 1

You discover that a popular beauty product (hairspray, lipstick,
perfume, deodorant, whatever you choose) is being used by
the manufacturer as a mind control device.

NOVEMBER 2

You spend several days sick in bed only to learn when you recover that you missed the news story of the century.

NOVEMBER 3

You slowly begin to suspect someone you work with just might be the devil.

NOVEMBER 4

Write a story that begins with someone standing on the deck of a ship, watching the sun rise over still waters.

NOVEMBER 5

While cleaning, you find a photograph of your spouse holding a newborn in the hospital, but it isn't one of your children.

NOVEMBER 6

You begin to suspect your roommate is trying to kill you.

NOVEMBER 7

You pick up a book at a bookstore or library,
and on your way to the counter to purchase it or check it out,
a note falls out of it.

NOVEMBER 8

Someone has locked themselves in your bathroom. Why?

NOVEMBER 9

Write a story that opens with someone taking a sleeping pill, but who then has to stay awake for some reason.

NOVEMBER 10

You used to be in a once-popular band and decide, years later, that you should get the guys back together again for a new album and tour. The problem is you haven't kept in touch with any of them over the years, and one of the members is now a celebrity in his or her own right.

NOVEMBER 11

You know something bad is going to happen and are powerless to stop it, but you still have to try.

NOVEMBER 12

While visiting a nursing home, you meet an elderly person who claims to be you from the future.

NOVEMBER 13

You're having a yard sale when the police show up.

NOVEMBER 14

Without looking or going outside or reading the weather forecast, you already know it's raining or is going to rain. Describe how you know.

NOVEMBER 15

Write a story about someone who is temporarily blinded.

NOVEMBER 16

Someone is tailgating another person at high speed on the interstate. Write the scene twice, once from each person's point of view.

NOVEMBER 17

Write a story about someone who has an escape plan ready to implement.

NOVEMBER 18

In the mail you receive a check for a large sum of money
from someone you don't know.
The check is made payable to you, but doesn't say why.

NOVEMBER 19

You're at the grocery store when you realize
you left a candle burning back home.

NOVEMBER 20

Write a story about someone trying to make it in a job or career typically dominated by the opposite gender.

NOVEMBER 21

You wake in the middle of the night to find
flashing lights filling your room.
They're from emergency response vehicles
silently parked on your street.
Pulling on a robe, you go out to investigate.

NOVEMBER 22

Write about two people who supposedly hate each other…and that's just what they want everyone else to think.

NOVEMBER 23

Write about someone who is going skydiving for the first time.

NOVEMBER 24

Write a story about someone who isn't going to make it home for the holidays from the point of view of the one person who really hopes they'll show up.

NOVEMBER 25

Write about someone celebrating an American Thanksgiving dinner for the first time.

NOVEMBER 26

While cleaning out the attic or basement, you find
an old diary or photograph that reminds you
of your first childhood crush or love.

NOVEMBER 27

You're the first person to arrive at your place of employment
one day, only to find something terribly wrong or out of place.

NOVEMBER 28

You're very upset about something and can't wait to confide in your spouse (or lover, roommate, or friend), but when they arrive, they're obviously very happy about something they can't wait to share with you.

NOVEMBER 29

Write a story from the point of view of a mythological creature who runs into or meets a human for the first time.

NOVEMBER 30

Why would someone be wearing a wedding gown
but not be getting married?

ꕥ

DECEMBER 1

You find a listing on Craig's List for someone giving away a pair of tickets to a local concert because they don't have anyone else to go with. You agree to take the tickets off their hands, but when you meet up, you're surprised to find the person is someone you've wanted to go out with for a while now, so you suggest you go to the show together. Describe your evening.

DECEMBER 2

Write a story that begins with someone going to see a lawyer.

DECEMBER 3

You're in one of the stalls in the restroom at work when two coworkers come in to gossip…without realizing you can overhear everything they're saying.

DECEMBER 4

Why would someone text while driving,
even if they knew it was dangerous?

DECEMBER 5

You ask a friend or lover to tell you the story of how they got
an oddly shaped scar.

DECEMBER 6

Every day you pick up a child from school (your own child or a relative, or someone you babysit). One day you're a little late arriving. When you get there, the child is gone.

DECEMBER 7

You find a ticket stub in your pocket for a show or even you don't remember attending.

DECEMBER 8

Write about someone who has prophetic dreams
after eating a particular food.

DECEMBER 9

You're winning big at the casino and are going to cash in your chips and call it a night when someone who's been watching you for a while approaches.

DECEMBER 10

Write a story about someone who finds
a frightening lump somewhere on their body.

DECEMBER 11

You go with a friend or relative to an audition
you secretly know they can't possibly win.

DECEMBER 12

You wake one morning to find several feet of snow on the ground…and it's still coming down.

ନଓ

DECEMBER 13

You often worry you forgot to lock your front door when you go out. One day you really *do* forget, and come home to find the door open.

DECEMBER 14

Write a story about someone who accidentally finds the Christmas gift another person is going to give them.

ഇ ന്ദ

DECEMBER 15

Two people with very different family holiday traditions celebrate their first Christmas together.

DECEMBER 16

Write a story that begins with someone losing a tooth.

DECEMBER 17

You've been tasked with scheduling your office Christmas dinner. You choose an exclusive local restaurant and have already settled on the menu and made the reservations. But when you call a few days before the event to confirm everything, the restaurant has gone out of business.

DECEMBER 18

Write a story from the point of view of a child's imaginary friend.

DECEMBER 19

You kiss someone you shouldn't under the mistletoe.

DECEMBER 20

Retell the familiar story of *Rudolph, the Red-Nosed Reindeer* from the point of view of one of the other reindeers on Santa's team.

ഇ ഒ

DECEMBER 21

You meet Santa Claus—the *real* Santa—as an adult for the second time in your life.

DECEMBER 22

You bring someone home to meet your family over the holidays…and you have an announcement to make.

DECEMBER 23

Write about someone spending the holidays away from home for the first time.

DECEMBER 24

At a holiday party, someone you hardly know comes up to you and says, "I know your secret."

ജ്ജ

DECEMBER 25

As a child, you always wanted on particular present you never got. Write a story in which you receive this childhood desire as a gift now as an adult.

DECEMBER 26

You try to return an unwanted gift, but run into the person who gave it to you while at the store.

DECEMBER 27

Write a story about what Santa Claus, Mrs. Claus, or the elves do after Christmas is over.

DECEMBER 28

Write about someone visiting a part of the world
where the sun doesn't shine for six months out of the year.

DECEMBER 29

Now that the holidays are over, you're happy the day
has come for your relatives to go home.
But something comes up that prevents them from leaving.

DECEMBER 30

You're cleaning up after the holidays when you find a gift you forgot to give someone.

DECEMBER 31

Because you don't want to break your New Year's resolution too soon, you rush to do something before the clock strikes midnight. What?

ABOUT THE AUTHOR

J.M. SNYDER LIVES in Richmond, Virginia. A graduate of George Mason University, Snyder is a multi-published, best-selling author of gay erotic and romantic fiction who has worked with several e-publishers, most notably Amber Allure Press, eXcessica, and Torquere Press. Snyder's short stories have appeared online and in anthologies by Alyson Books, Cleis Press, and others.

In 2010, Snyder started JMS Books LLC to publish her own writing as well as fiction, nonfiction, and poetry she enjoys.

Positive feedback as well as hate mail can be forwarded to the author at jms@jmsnyder.net.

CPSIA information can be obtained at www.ICGtesting.com
Printed in the USA
LVOW050400020213

318337LV00013B/304/P